"To summarize Byron's influence on the digital revolution requires new terminology. He would be best described as an 'Extrapreneur'... a man with more ideas, revelations, and insight into all things 'web' than any entrepreneur I've ever met. Hitching a ride on the Byron Express means a high-velocity journey into the undefined territory where opportunity and discovery meet."

—*Phin Gay, Principal, Direct Results Group, Inc.*

"Content marketing is the future of marketing, and Byron is right in the middle of the mix, helping to lead the conversation. Byron knows content inside and out, and shares his vast experience in this book. Just a few minutes engaging in this content and you'll have more ideas than you can shake a stick at."

—*Joe Pulizzi, Founder, Content Marketing Institute*

"Byron White knows content—like myself, he built his business with it. He understands the value that content can bring to your business. If you don't take the 60 minutes to read these tips, don't worry about it—your competitor will. Let me give you a quick tip: Buy this book and put its content to work for your business."

—*Bryan Eisenberg, Founder & CMO, IdealSpot*

International Standard Book Number: 978-1-60275-057-9

*This book is intended for use as an informational guide and entertainment
purposes and should not be used as a substitute for any professional medical care
or treatment, professional legal advice or professional financial guidance.*

CONTENTS

Foreword

Saying content is king is the equivalent of saying money is valuable; it's true, but obvious. But is all content equally valuable? Of course not! What makes content valuable is its relevance to your readers. How that message is delivered is what continually evolves.

I often ask marketers to define content. Unfortunately, this critical question often goes unexplored. If you ask most marketers, they'll tell you that it's the copy on a website. While this answer is certainly true, it's inadequate—content is more than just copy.

The answers to this question are numerous and nuanced, but a good place to start is to think of web content as the public conversation that takes place between you and the visitor, whether that conversation is one-way (from you to the visitor), two-way (between the visitor and you), or shared among visitors.

The more this content causes, persuades, or woosW visitors to take a profitable action, the more valuable it is. If it doesn't do this, it's more like bad entertainment. Using content as a marketing tool is obvious for those who have compelling intellectual property, but it isn't just for those types anymore; almost any company or service can find a content marketing strategy that will work.

Bryan Eisenberg, Founder & CMO, IdealSpot

A Note from Byron White

What is content marketing? It's the art of listening to your customers' needs and wants and the science of delivering it to them in a compelling, engaging way. It's constantly testing campaigns with A/B testing to learn what works best. And it's a simple, well-told story that gets passed around and keeps readers coming back for more.

In the past ten years, I've led a team that has created more than 18 million words for 500 clients. We created LifeTips.com from scratch and it now drives more than one million monthly readers without any advertising or marketing spend. We've screened hundreds of writers and put them to the test and we've learned what works with landing page optimization.

The secret to content marketing is great writers. If you hire great writers, you will grow your marketing and sales at an accelerated rate. If you hire lousy writers, you'll remain stagnant with content that simply does not connect with readers or the search engines and be forced to feed the pipeline of sales with traditional marketing that will eventually become extinct.

Enjoy these tips, which will open up a new pipeline of business. You'll find great ideas, uplifting examples, insider tips, and SEO secrets and methods to measure the ROI you demand from this book and from your content marketing investment.

Byron White

Content Planning

The Content Plan

From 2005 to 2010, we developed dozens of content plans for a wide variety of clients. We asked the fundamental questions that were necessary for our clients' content marketing success:

- How much content do I need to publish to impact my business?

- How frequently do I need to publish content to achieve my goals?

- What distribution channels should I use to maximize success?

- How do I measure the impact and return on my investment?

When you ask these questions for your own organization, the answers become the essence of a Content Plan. The more money you plan to spend on content marketing, the more planning and analysis you need to achieve your goals.

Complex plans require hundreds of hours of research and development. Even simple plans take time. Follow the tips and advice in this section and you'll hit all the key elements for success.

02

Keyword Research

Content strategy typically aims at driving more traffic to a website and generating more leads for sales. Researching keywords to target for search engine optimization requires developing a keyword universe (KU). Your KU should have a balance of high volume, high PPC keywords, and long tail, low volume, low PPC price keywords.

Depending on the competitive nature of your business and your budget, you select keywords that align with the amount of content you plan on creating. Use tools like SpyFu.com to harvest keywords and export them to a spreadsheet, along with the key information, including PPC price, search volume, difficulty rating and more. Start sorting keywords by those variables to find the keywords that you want to target for SEO.

03

Keyword Research Tools

See the special Keyword Tool appendix for the full list of resources. As mentioned, Spyfu.com is a great tool to help you quickly find all of the keywords that drive traffic to your competition. You can also find keyword gaps or overlaps, and compare your success to that of the competition.

In minutes, you can use SEO tools to find those keywords that matter for your business. Free trials enable you to get started quickly, with no up-front cost.

Developing Keyword Silos

What's a Topic Map? What's a Keyword Silo? And why do I need them?

Topic Maps, created by writers or content strategists, are driven by the wants and needs of readers and fans. Keyword Silos are groups of keywords you compile from the keyword universe SEO specialists created for your project.

Topic Maps and Keyword Silos eventually need to align to make it easy to both generate and optimize content. Then you can group keywords by topic, products, services or other shared characteristics. Find the balance and harmony that appeal to both SEO specialists and Content Strategists, as well as your readers and the search engines.

Define Your Goals

Content marketing is like a team sport that requires everyone to be on the same page: Digital strategists, SEO specialists, writers, editors and more. The first questions you need to ask are, "What is the purpose of the content we're going to create; why are we creating it; and how will we measure its success?"

Content Strategy goals include conversion, traffic increases, improved listing positions, time on site (stickiness), repeat visitation, downloads, subscription, increased sales and more. See the final performance measurement section of this book to review all alternative goals and pick those that make sense for your company to focus on given your budget, time and resources.

Competitive Intelligence

Develop a quick assessment of how you stack up against the competition. It's fast, easy and important to get the big picture.

First, create a spreadsheet with your site and your competition as column headers. Then create the following categories: Traffic, PPC Spend, Content Portfolio, Link Popularity, Publishing Frequency, Facebook Reach, Twitter Reach, LinkedIn Reach, Testimonials, Strategic Partnership, Internal Links, SEO Strength, Search Performance, A/B Testing and any other evaluators that make sense.

Next, grade your site against the competition using the various tools that offer the answers in minutes. Your overall score will begin to tell you how difficult (and expensive) it will be to capture organic market share with content marketing.

07

Personas

Who is your audience? Develop personas that pinpoint the wants and needs of your readers and customers. Personas help your writers understand what style and tone will connect with readers and keep them coming back for more.

Use demographic analytics and SEO tools to learn more about your audience. Speak with as many customers as you can to get a feel for their DNA. In the end, create three or four personas that reflect specific, recognizable characteristics, habits and motivation patterns for each. Two of my favorites are ADD Andy and Sophisticated Sally, who each require different types of content at different points in the buy cycle.

Style Guide and the X Factor

When you take the leap of faith to put content marketing at the center of your brand, you'll need a style guide that defines who you are and what you stand for. What is your X factor that will help distinguish you from the pack of competition?

Style guides vary from company to company but typically include do's and don'ts for content creation and optimization. In addition, a style guide should include a clear definition of who the target audience is and how content should be presented in order to maximize engagement.

Here a just a few examples of writing styles:

- Authoritative tone that helps solidify your leadership position

- Innovative flavor that offers new energy, surprise and delight

- Lean approach that gets to the point by chopping the fat

- Entertaining spurts that motivate readers to find the next plug

- Storytelling that unravels the message all the way to the end

- Personal insight that connects deeply with pain points and solutions

2016 Content Plan

Sure, you can spend many months and thousands of dollars on creating a content plan. Years ago, we had to "prove" that content marketing was the right choice for marketing spend. Content plans helped "make the case" for content marketing with predictions on ROIs.

Now, things have changed. Forward thinking companies understand they must publish information readers want and need—content assets that get passed around and shared. Focusing on creating that great content should now be the plan. Find out what works for your readers and customers. Start writing and publishing content now, and plan along the way. The new plan is: Plan less and invest in high quality content that performs.

To be successful with content marketing, you need to publish a steady stream of content that engages readers and keeps them coming back for more.

Content Creation

10

Earning Trust

Earning trust is the ultimate goal of content marketing—and it's not easy. Start by listening to your customers and asking them questions. Discover their problems and supply the solutions they need. Make sure that the content you create is something that customers can believe and that it offers guidance and advice in a meaningful way. This type of information will build trust in your company as a solution provider and eventually lead to the sale.

Next, stop talking and start listening. Talking too much about your company, your product features and benefits, and your exceptional services and awards is guaranteed to turn off customers. Your customers demand educational content without the marketing spin. Cut back on the self-promotional speak and earn trust with your customers with quality information that's readily available online.

Finally, get active. Products are static things, but solutions are active answers to challenges your prospective clients care about. Make the transformation: Feature content on your product pages that specifies how your products can solve problems. You'll reach prospects at the right place and time—when they're considering a purchase—so you can expect your conversions to skyrocket!

11

Great Content from Great Writers

Great content is more than just useful information—it's compelling, entertaining writing that hooks readers and keeps them coming back for more. After all, searchers and browsers are readers. So a successful content marketing strategy begins with great writers who know how to craft a story and tell it well.

In the review process, ask writers to show you content that's more than just useful information. If they don't have it, ask for one short sample of content that will connect with you in a certain way. Screen freelance writers' work carefully before hiring, and only hire the best. You'll be doing your readers—and your business—a favor.

12

Go for Quality

You have an obligation to evaluate the usefulness of your content to readers. Trim out the fat regularly, especially if you can replace the fluff with good stuff. If your website offers interesting information, quality product or service descriptions, and helpful advice that solves problems, you are already on your way to increasing traffic. While search engines may be tricked by search engine optimization (SEO) strategies that are geared toward increasing rankings rather than providing a quality website, victory is not so sweet when the readership time on your site decreases as a result of poor content. "Be the ball," as they say. If your visitors are not impressed with your content, you'll never win the war of words on the web.

Great content is clear, simple, and easy to understand. Can you say the same for the messages you send out? Or do they require an explanation from your sales reps? People won't act on information that they don't understand. Trim the fat and KISS—keep it simple, stupid. Turn perplexing problems into tidy tidbits of information that help you communicate effectively.

13

Beware the Bias

Turning your company's website into a "destination" site for your target audience is an ambitious goal. Why? Readers view information sites created by companies as "biased" and therefore less valuable. If possible, create intellectual articles and videos from industry leaders outside your company to help validate your commitment to knowledge vs. sales. Offer free tools that solve problems on the fly and remove all promotions within any rich content to confirm your commitment to thought leadership.

14

Shorter is Better for the Web

Short paragraphs of three to five sentences are ideal for web content. Readers are looking for information quickly, which is why most of them find longer paragraphs unappealing. Shorter paragraphs can be scanned quickly and allow readers to determine if they want to continue reading your website. Keep in mind that, while shorter paragraphs may entice readers to stay on your website for longer, they will soon leave if your content lacks interesting and accurate information. Keep it short and keep your customers.

One way to keep your content easy to read and scan is to use bullet points to highlight key points in your articles and to give readers a good overview of what the article covers. Easy-to-read text on your website will keep visitors interested in your content and returning to see what's new, and your search engine placements can benefit from providing content that is appealing to readers.

Content Marketing Assets A–Z

15

Articles

Some customers want all the juicy details. In order to appeal to this kind of reader, consider using longer, more thorough articles instead of short tips and bullet lists.

While articles are particularly appropriate for more complex subject matter, don't lose sight of the end goal: to take a boring subject and make it palatable. Just because it's long doesn't mean that it can't be an entertaining read.

16

Blogs

When done right, blogging is a great way to earn trust and drive sales. Our experience shows that blogs need to be created and maintained by your company's leaders.

Start by educating your leaders on the fundamentals (if necessary). Next, you'll need to reach out and start conversations on the web. Deploy a steady stream of engaging posts combined with posts on other sites, and your corporate blog will soon be attracting readers and supporting sales.

17

Books

It's amazing what having your name on the cover of a book can do. After all, authors are authorities. A book with your name and/or your company's name on it gives you visibility and credibility. On-demand publishing makes it affordable and easy; books can be shipped and distributed one copy at a time, which allows you to test your book's business-building potential with split testing and multivariate testing.

18

Brochures

Well-written brochures translate your company's expertise and point of view into knowledge that people want and need. They show people what your company can do for them and how it can help them solve problems and make life better. When created effectively, brochures sell without selling and instead focus on solving problems creatively with headlines, images, and descriptions that readers find compelling and engaging.

19

Case Studies

Case studies help prospective customers evaluate the features and benefits of what you offer by showing them your current clients' positive experiences with your products, people, and services. Develop case studies with your prospective customers' needs and wants in mind and jazz them up with informational graphics and good design. Show them not only how you solve problems, but also how you delivered the ROI your clients demand.

E-books

Web readers are orbiting at high speeds and are difficult to move down the sales funnel. An e-book download will help catch them on the fly, induce trial, and showcase your experience. Offering information in an e-book associates your brand with something that solves problems, enlightens, and entertains.

E-books also offer motivation for sales, and offering free PDF downloads in exchange for action on your website helps improve conversions. An e-book takes your brand offline and puts it into the hands of prospective customers. It's a cost effective solution that offers measurable returns.

eBrochures

In terms of content, an eBrochure is almost the same as the more conventional brochure described above; however, publishing brochures electronically has several benefits. For one thing, it eliminates the costs of printing and shipping. Also, and perhaps more importantly, it allows you to make your brochure more interactive. Add live links that will direct readers to your website to learn even more about your products and services.

Infographics

Hourly, or even by the minute, we're bombarded with tons of information from a wide variety of sources that seem to multiply every day. Infographics are aimed at making all of this information more digestible. The term tends to conjure images of numbers, arrows, scientific solutions, and charts; however, like most content marketing disciplines, the delivery has changed, and interactive visualizations are taking the design field by storm.

By distilling complex information, establishing a hierarchy, and isolating what's important, infographics cause the essence of the material to float to the top where it can be identified, read, mentally stored, and even passed around by web readers. When executed properly, infographics help drive traffic and sales.

Manuals

Here's a challenge for any great writer: Take the usual boring manual that gets handed over after a sale and turn it into a guide full of useful, entertaining tips and advice. A guide like that won't gather dust on top of a filing cabinet, but will be consulted over and over again.

Microsites

Creating a website on a focused topic helps readers really dig into the full story, and including words, images, video, white papers, guides, mobile feeds, and RSS feeds offers greater opportunities for engagement and means of measuring success. Microsites also allow you to optimize certain phrases for the search engines to drive traffic from a wider pool of long-tail keyword phrases that are based on a particular theme. Landing page optimization services are much easier to deploy site-wide, which means that it's easy to test their business-building potential.

Newsletters

Newsletters give you the opportunity to demonstrate your company's expertise to customers, prospective customers, and opt-in subscribers on a regular basis; they're a great way to stay at top-of-mind with customers and prospects who matter. Keep the content easy to read and scan by offering short tips that your readers can use and integrate them creatively with information related to your products and services. Make your newsletter a must-read by publishing information on what's new in your industry.

Podcasts

Audio is a powerful marketing tool for a couple of reasons. First of all, it allows you to catch your readers (or in this case, listeners) while they're on the go. Imagine having listeners checking iTunes for new episodes of your podcast and listening to them on the train ride home. Or what about mailing iPods loaded with your podcasts to 100 of your prospective clients?

Second of all, audio communicates emotion much more effectively than text. This means that your audience will get a much clearer idea of your company's corporate personality by listening to you than they would by reading from a screen, and having a personality humanizes your company and helps establish trust.

The great thing is that with new technology that's easy to travel with, recording and publishing podcasts has never been easier, even while you're on the go.

Presentation Slides

Slide sharing is a great way to join the thought leadership bandwagon. SlideShare.net, SlideRocket.com, and dozens of other communities allow you to get your thoughts out in presentation form and the views in—for free. For full impact, add audio to your slides and offer the full story in animated form. Great presentations get passed around and shared, so join the fun.

RSS and XML Feeds

Get the words out and the traffic in with RSS and XML feeds
that keep readers interested with a steady stream of new and
appealing content. Learn which posts inspire RSS subscriptions,
and create more content in the same vein. Make it easy for
readers to subscribe with best practice buttons and logos,
and encourage social bookmarks on content along with feed
subscriptions. Also, post social recognition and votes in order
to build trust and entice subscriptions.

Social Media

These days, putting the power of social media to work for
your business is critical for online success. To use social media
effectively, you'll need both technical and editorial support.
The new social media universe offers a variety of platforms
with which to reach your target audience, including Twitter,
Facebook, LinkedIn, corporate blogging, and more. Define
success not by the number of followers or subscribers you
accumulate, but instead by the number of conversations about
your content that are launched as a result of your efforts.

Tip and Advice Centers

What's your website missing? Chances are, it's a section that translates your company's expertise and point of view into easy-to-understand tips, pointers, and advice that people can really use. Tips do the most important job marketing can do—they show people what your company can do for them. You need expert writers to create about 100 tips to appeal to readers and the search engines, and internal links need to be crafted to properly support SEO. The ROI you demand will be visible in new search engine traffic from specific keyword phrases, as well as conversions from lead generation features such as e-book downloads and product service nders. A Tip and Advice Center will offer the SEO edge you need to get ahead of your competition.

Video

Your audience has broadband and probably watches two to ten YouTube videos each month. Site, sound, and motion are becoming the presentation media of choice for companies that are in the know. So why are you still presenting plain HTML content?

The good news is that you don't need a Hollywood production team to get the video out and the viewers in—yet. Purchasing an HD camcorder and a good microphone will get you moving in the right direction. Combine that with the essential, well-told story and you'll join the video revolution.

White Papers

There's nothing like a white paper to establish your company's expertise and authority. No matter how technical the subject, the goal is to make the content understandable. You'll want to subtly infuse the document with your company's corporate personality to make the paper unmistakably yours. Then, go crazy and add some visuals, motivating headlines, and humor to entertain along the way. Knowledge is power, especially if it gets talked about and shared on the web.

Widgets

Let's face it—web surfers expect to be entertained these days. Entertain them with Test Widgets that engage readers and keep them coming back for more challenges. Have expert writers craft multiple-choice questions that challenge the skill and knowledge of readers in topics that relate to your products and services. Incorrect answers trigger correct explanations that inform, educate, and sell. Find free online resources to build widgets easily.

Webinars

In contrast to webcasts that are typically one-way transmissions
of data, webinars—web-hosted seminars—offer the dual ability
to present information in a lecture or workshop format, while also
allowing for interaction with the audience via discussion groups
or forums. Today's well-designed webinars leap over traditional
barriers like distance and time by allowing interested viewers to
take part with minimal impact on scheduling and travel.

Workbooks

A workbook is another great way to build your brand by offering
readers information and advice that they're interested in.
Workbook downloads are proven to motivate sales and improve
conversion rates. Why not take that PowerPoint presentation
and turn it into a PDF workbook that's easy to download and
pass around? Create content that offers keen insight that your
competition hesitates to disclose and find opportunities to
engage readers with challenges that educate. It's very important
to choose topics that are interesting and that offer the thought
leadership associated with your brand.

Hiring Great Writers

36

Mediocrity is Expensive

Cheaper is just cheaper. When you have a limited budget for marketing, it's natural to ask, "How can I get this project done in the least expensive way?" But remember: You get what you pay for. Sure, your brother's kid might be able to turn out some content for your website—and cheaply—but will it sell your product? Will it resonate with the people most likely to buy from you? Will it be a professional, appealing representation of your organization? If you just need your customers to find your phone number and directions to your store, the inexpensive solution may be OK. If not, find freelance writers who have the professional experience and talent you need.

37

Pick Writers with Expertise

Who is your customer most interested in talking to? Probably your product experts and customer service people. Develop content that answers your customers' product and service questions and have your employees use your content in their conversations with customers. Content that solves problems and answers questions in a genuine voice will do more to engage customers and grow your business.

Finding Freelance Writers

Hint: He's the pale, thin guy chained to his computer. Whether you're looking for a freelance writer to hire or you're a freelancer looking for work, there are plenty of freelance sites online that match professionals with companies. Employers can search specific positions and scan writers' resumes, and freelancers can seek out work that companies have posted. Full-time, in-house employment sites work similarly to freelance sites. Some freelance employment sites also act as go-betweens, helping to sort out payment issues and common questions about the freelance hiring process.

Keep the Peace in Your Relationship

Freelance relationships go more smoothly when you, the client, go into them prepared. Before you place an advertisement or hire someone for freelance content writing jobs, you should be ready to answer these questions:

- What specific work do you want the writer to do?

- What is the goal of the work?

- How does this project fit into your company's goals?

- What expertise is needed to do this work properly?

- What is the budget for this project?

- What is the deadline for this project?

- What is your plan for revisions and extras that may come up?

Interviewing Writers

Here are some answers about questions. Developing good questions for a job interview is an art form; you have to know what to ask that will help you decide if someone is right for a position—without overstepping your boundaries and asking things that are inappropriate. Be very careful that you don't ask questions that could be interpreted as discriminatory.

Below are a few of our favorite interview questions that instantly offer insight into experience:

- "I reviewed your work, and really like the X piece. Could you tell me more about the assignment?"

- "What do you know about the target audience that you'd be writing for? How do you get under their skin?"

- "Has your work ever been tested with split testing or multivariate testing techniques? If so, what did you learn from the tests?"

- "How do you implement SEO in your content? What research tools do you use? Do you also create meta strategy for your clients? What about link strategy?"

A great way to get started writing questions for an interview is to use the job description. For example, if you are looking to hire a freelance SEO writer, write out a list of questions based on the freelance SEO writer description and then narrow things down. You don't have to cover every point, but be sure that the main areas are touched on. Try to ask open-ended questions that give writers a chance to explain their thoughts. Avoid yes or no answers.

Talking the Talk

When in Rome, speak like a Roman. Before anyone writes
for your website, make sure he or she has a firm grasp of the
vernacular used in your industry. Make lists of well-known
words and phrases that are used in the industry, and make sure
that any freelance writer you hire uses them in your content.
Research proves that you can connect better with readers
(and spider bots) if your language is matched to your industry.
So let any prospective freelance content writers know that
it's mandatory to learn and understand the lingo so that the
content they create will resonate with your readers.

Managing Work-at-Home Freelancers

Can you handle a long-distance relationship? You may be
understandably leery of hiring a freelance content writer who
works hundreds or even thousands of miles from your company.
How will you know that they're really working on your project or
that they'll do it the right way? Ideas for handling this well include:

- Delivery. Start with one project with a defined
  delivery date and see how it goes.

- Instant Messaging. Surprisingly, most freelancers
  like IM check-ins. This shows that you care.

- Home Office Setup Confirmation. Check for the
  latest dedicated home office gear.

- Remote Employment References. Ask about the
  workflow and delivery patterns.

- Follow Up. Check in often to see how things are
  going, especially early on in the project.

Set the Communication Plan

A good freelance web writer will ask at the beginning of your relationship how you prefer to communicate (phone, email, IM, meetings, etc.), what kind of updates you want on progress and how often, and who he or she should contact in case questions or problems should arise.

If the freelancer doesn't ask, run like hell. Just kidding. But do provide this information as part of your plan for success. Good communication is vital to a successful freelance relationship. Weekly check-in is standard with our freelancers, either via email or a brief phone discussion.

Setting the expectations for communication can have a surprising impact on the quality of the work. Good writers want to exceed your expectations, so let them know what they are.

Training Freelancers

Training can make a big difference in the quality of the work a freelancer turns out. Understanding your company's culture and style is hard for a stranger to your business. Take the time not just to talk about the project, but also to discuss the philosophy, chemistry, and environment that you work in, as this will help the writer to craft messages to your audience. Consider setting up quick, twenty-minute meetings with any of the following employees at your company:

- Existing writers and editors who create content on similar projects

- Experts in your industry who know about your company

- Customers who use your products or services

- Sales manager or sales representatives at your company

- Customer service manager who discusses customer needs regularly

45

Paying Freelance Writers

We recommend using money. Freelance SEO writers, like any vendors, should get paid in correlation to their agreed-upon rates, based on a number of variables that can include experience, difficulty of the job, importance of the job, readership, impact on your company, and other factors discussed, negotiated, and agreed upon contractually by both parties. It can be difficult to assess all of the variables and determine a fair price. Flexible plans that delay or ignore this obligation create a lose-lose situation for both parties. Quality satisfaction can also be considered in the contractual obligations; a mediator or third party can resolve any disagreement over the quality or quantity of the work performed.

In the end, the obligation should be on the freelance writer and his or her writing contracts to make provisions for these cases, assessing a "kill fee" (usually half the contracted rate) if a project is completed but not used and a late fee for the client who delays payment. There should also be a penalty for the freelancer if he or she delivers late.

If a freelancer or a freelance agency asks you for these provisions, don't be alarmed. They indicate that you're more likely to be working with an experienced professional—and therefore more likely to get good value for your money.

You need to optimize content for both readers AND the search engines. And that's the art and science that drives content marketing.

Content Optimization

Best Practice Content Optimization

46

Keep it Fresh

Keeping your content fresh can help you increase your search engine placements. Some website owners obtain high search engine rankings but then make the mistake of not changing their website for fear of negatively impacting their rankings. This strategy is faulty because it is fresh content that keeps visitors coming back to your website. Try adding fresh content at least once per month; you should see the impact of a steady stream of new content by the second month of deployment, and this can easily be tracked.

47

Don't Duplicate. Don't Duplicate.

Whether or not popular search engines have a penalty for duplicate content is under debate in the SEO community. Some argue that it is merely a myth, while others testify that they have seen a tremendous boost in ratings by simply replacing any duplicated content in question. One of the main reasons search engines may impose a duplicate content penalty is to avoid serving up nearly identical pages in their rankings, as this is not useful to those who use the search engine and may cause people to opt for a different search engine.

To be on the safe side, create original content on your website and place a copyright notice on your website restricting others from using your content. Next, filter any content you publish on your website with duplicate content checking technology. Also, frequently search for duplicate content on your website and take action if you find issues. Don't worry about content that other sites may have copied from your website—you can use Google's archive dates to help determine publishing dates.

48

Get in the Know About SEO

The web is filled with plenty of content that is related to SEO. Searching for phrases such as "SEO strategies," "SEO techniques," "SEO tips," or similar terms will yield countless results. When using the internet for research, pay attention to the dates associated with the information you find, as SEO has changed throughout the years and articles written just a few years ago may be very outdated. The benefit of using the internet to research SEO is that websites that are ranked high in the search engines are skilled at SEO and are therefore likely to provide quality information.

Follow the Leaders

One way to learn SEO techniques is to study other websites that rank well in the search engines. As you review these websites, make note of what you really like about them. This might include the colors, fonts, content, services or products available, or anything else that catches your eye. This is important because what you like about this particular website is likely to be enjoyed by other readers as well. The search engines are aware of the characteristics that appeal to the masses, and they reward these websites with high rankings, so look and learn.

If at First You Don't Succeed...

Practice, trial and error cannot be overestimated when it comes to SEO. Once you launch and optimize your website, it takes time to evaluate the results of your efforts. If you find that your search engine rankings are lower than expected, it's time to start experimenting with different strategies. Try only changing one variable at a time so that you can determine which variable helps to increase or decrease your rankings. If you make too many changes at once, it might be difficult to determine what has affected your site's rankings. Prove your ability to achieve top listings with super long tail keyword phrases you use in the content on a page, title tag, meta keywords, and meta descriptions, then build some internal links within your site to that page using that phrase.

You Need Friends

Tap into your friends in the SEO industry and learn from them. Ask for a one-hour meeting to learn how they deploy SEO solutions to clients. Seeing the workflow process will help you understand the big picture and what's necessary for success. Those in the industry are much more likely to share some of the tricks of the trade with friends or family members than with others in the industry. Fantastic free tools for learning and experimentation combined with some insider knowledge and wisdom will give you all you need to optimize content for the web or take your writing career to the next level.

Work the Trade Shows

One way to learn about SEO is to set up a consultation with an SEO firm at one of the free trade shows in the industry. Hearing the pitch of an experienced SEO firm can teach you a great deal about the process of optimizing a website. Many trade shows are free and all of them will expose you to dozens of SEO firms that can offer advice right on the show floor.

Some trade shows offer SEO conferences and seminars as well. Many SEO seminars may be too detailed for those with no SEO knowledge, but there are some seminars that are specifically for novices; when choosing a seminar, pay attention to the level of diffculty of the material to be covered. If you know the basics, look for intermediate level courses. Check out Search Engine Strategies, PubCon, ad:tech, and other shows in the search engine marketing industry.

It Never Ends

You'll never be done with your SEO work. You have to accept this when you begin any SEO project in order to avoid frustration, disappointment, or confusion. SEO isn't something that you can do just once and declare done; rather, SEO is one of the most complex areas of online marketing and must be worked on regularly and treated as a process, with techniques being tested and revised constantly. Find tracking technology that will allow you to manage the performance of your SEO skills, performance of the website, and success or failure of specific keyword phrases.

You can never guarantee that top listing positions will result from your SEO efforts. Any such claim by anyone is an instant declaration of SEO ignorance. Placement in "natural language" or free search (the listings on the left-hand side of most search results) can't be guaranteed because the formulas used to rank sites are secret and constantly changing. Companies may be able to guarantee ranking using pay-per-click ads, but this is a different thing entirely. So, when you get in tune with SEO skills, beware of false promises and specific rankings. Instead, get in tune with best practice knowledge about how to optimize content for the search engines with specific keywords targeted for the campaign, supporting an overall SEO strategy.

Be a Joiner

You can learn a lot about SEO by joining online forums or email lists where users exchange SEO information. This is an excellent resource for novice website owners who want to ask questions about strategies for SEO. The responses you receive can be insightful. Also, if you choose an active forum, you will likely receive multiple opinions on any given topic and be privy to debates on different strategies.

Deep, Dark Secrets

SEO is a complex task because the criteria used to rank sites are confidential. The ranking formula used by each search engine is that company's most valuable intellectual property, so they don't reveal it. There are around 200 criteria used to rank sites and the exact weight that is given to each item is never revealed. To make matters even more complicated, the weight that's given to these items changes regularly in order to deal with advances in search and optimization techniques. As a result, adhering to best practices is always going to get you better long-term results than flavor-of-the-month SEO. Go with the tried and true.

Don't Overdo It

Writers with new SEO tools often overwork SEO for a website. Keep it simple for success in the search engines. Content on your website should be related to the overall theme of your website. It should also be written in straightforward language that is easy for readers to follow.

Best practice keyword density is largely debatable. Many SEO experts consider 2 to 20% an appropriate range, and most agree that overuse of keywords (that is, exceeding 20%) is not an effective strategy for SEO success. Most search engines can detect when keywords are not being used logically and your website might be banned if caught using keywords unnaturally. Also, stuffing keywords will not look natural to readers. If your content is relevant to the keywords that you optimize for, you will naturally use the words repeatedly and will achieve a density that does not appear forced. Check your content with a keyword density tool to confirm that you're not using a particular keyword excessively. Easy does it.

The Meta Keyword Debate

At one time, having the right meta keywords was the key to SEO success. Not any more. As search engines and their ranking techniques have gotten more complex, meta keywords have taken on less importance in good SEO; however, it is still very important that they be used wisely and effectively. Although more than 30 meta keywords are technically allowed, for best practice, select only five to eight keywords per page, relevant to the content on the page. Bear in mind that Google has published documents stating that its algorithm does not factor in meta keywords when determining listing positions. But every inch counts!

Descriptive tags also fall into the debate camp of effort vs. reward, but creating meta descriptions along with all meta data is best practice and imperative to SEO. Some argue that search engines disregard meta tags in their search algorithms, but no one makes the case that you may be penalized for optimizing tags. Evidence suggests that Google publishes the content of meta descriptions often in the actual search results that are displayed on the page.

The Spice of Life—and SEO

One mistake that novice optimizers make is not taking advantage of keyword variations, synonyms, and family keywords in optimization practice. Repeating the same keyword throughout your article may result in a high keyword density, but it might also be worthwhile to replace a few of those original keywords with variations of the keyword. While it is a good idea to do keyword research to determine which keywords are popular in search engines, it is also important to remember that not all internet users think alike. For example, a website on keyword variations should contain terms such as "keyword derivatives" or "keyword deviation," as these might be terms used by internet searchers. Fill your web content with keywords and variations of these keywords in a natural way, and your website will appeal to both readers and search engines.

Don't Forget Traditional Marketing

SEO specialists often put the blinders on to natural, organic growth on the web. Traditional online marketing with paid text ads, banner ads, affiliate marketing campaigns, email campaigns, and other online marketing initiatives complements and supports SEO efforts. Marketing can be an effective SEO strategy for both new websites that are preparing to launch and for existing websites that are looking to increase search engine rankings. This may seem like an unusual strategy for SEO, but marketing creates interest in your website, which can increase time-on-site visitation, traffic support and growth, and other factors that can trigger the algorithm to make the case for ranking improvement in the search engines. Basically, the art and science of SEO includes popularity on the web, which can be supported with online marketing.

Telltale Title Tags

Title tags help make a case for SEO success and continue to be part of best practice methods. For new- to-SEO readers, the title of your website does not refer to the text at the top of your website that is visible to viewers. The term "title" refers to the HTML code that is used to title your website and appears between the title tags in your website. This text is placed at the top of the internet browser and is also the automatic name that is given to the web page. Although this text does not appear directly on your website, it is viewable by search engines when they crawl your pages and your site. SEO specialists typically select two or three keywords for each page of the site that best match the content on the page.

ALT Tags are A-OK

The use of ALT tags is one SEO strategy that is often overlooked. Images on your website can create an excellent look that is aesthetically pleasing to readers, but unless you're utilizing your ALT tags, these images do not help increase your search engine rankings. Search engines do not view images as they crawl your web- site; however, if you apply ALT tags to your images, the search engines will see the text that is placed in these tags. This gives the website owner the opportunity to include a description of the image that incorporates relevant keywords.

62

Prominence Works

Prominence of your keywords can have an impact on your SEO. Prominence refers to where a keyword is located relative to the top of the website. Including your keywords in the title tags (which are visible to search engines) and in the website title (which is visible to readers) are two ways to increase your prominence for a particular keyword. Also, putting header tags around the visible title can make the keywords contained in this title appear more prominent.

63

Embed, and You're Dead

Embedded text or links should not be used in website design that is intended to rank well in search engines. This includes the use of coding to create text and links that are not visible to website viewers but are visible to search engines. This is considered a deceptive SEO strategy and is likely to be penalized upon discovery by search engines. For this reason, it is considered not only a waste of time, but an effort that can do more harm than good. Embedded text and links offer no value to your readers and can cause search engines to penalize your website.

Cloak, and You're Broke

Deceptive SEO strategies such as cloaking are viewed as "black hat" practice by the search engines and should be avoided at all costs. Cloaking involves serving websites that are specifically tailored for the IP address of the reader. The feature enables websites to serve one website to human readers and another to search engines. The technique may result in your website being penalized by search engines.

Link Love: Optimizing Links

65

Lovable Links

Having read Google's patent several times, it seems clear that in the foreseeable future, quality inbound links will continue to have the most impact on your search engine rankings and organic listing positions. Most of the search engine algorithms place some value on the amount and quality of inbound links that point toward your website. The ranking of the outside website that links to your own website factors into the amount of weight that search engines place on this inbound link when determining your rank—but don't confuse page rank with authority status. The best links come from popular websites that readers value and visit regularly. When popular, authoritative websites link to yours, you help make the case that your site is important and worthy of a top listing.

66

Evaluate Links Carefully

You can't judge a book by its cover, and you can't determine the link value of a website just by its Google Page Rank status, either. For a closer look at the deeper picture, check the Alexa rating of the site as well as the number of pages indexed at Google, Bing, and other search engines. It's essential to check back-link popularity as well.

Link Exchanges

One bad apple can spoil the whole bunch. Approach link exchanges with caution. Companies that do not comply with ethical linking standards can hurt your website if you link to them or if they link to you, so get the facts and perform some tests before you agree to a link exchange. Remember that link exchanges in general are farther down the link power chain and are less influential to your listing positions in the search engines.

Link Exclusivity

Research proves that link power is diminished as the number of links off a web page increases. Link power seems to be further reduced when competing websites receive links from the same site, so the best links are exclusive links to your website—links that your competition doesn't have. Find links that are off the beaten track; it's the secret to improving your listing positions in the search engines.

Directory Assistance

When optimizing your website, it's worthwhile to submit your website to directories such as Yahoo! and DMOZ. Directories significantly affect your search engine marketing. One way that they can help your website is through the increased traffic that they can provide. A listing in one of these directories will also help the search engines index your website.

Don't Forget a Sitemap

One of the do's of SEO is to create a sitemap for your website.
A sitemap is essentially a listing of all of the pages of your
website. It's typically stored in your robot.txt file located on
your home page. The reason a sitemap is important to SEO is
it enables the search engine to crawl all of the pages of your
website quickly and efficiently; however, care should be taken
to ensure that the sitemap does not contain broken links, as
they can cause the search engine to exit your website before
crawling the remainder of the pages.

If It's Broke, Fix It

Broken links on your website can be detrimental to your SEO.
One important step that should be taken in optimizing your
website is to test all of the links on your website to ensure that
they function properly. There
are two main reasons why broken links can negatively affect
your search engine rankings. First, broken links are extremely
frustrating to website visitors. Visitors may overlook one or two
broken links, but if you have more than that, they are likely to
exit your website quickly. Second, search engines will typically
automatically exit your website after encountering the first
broken link. If this happens on an early page of your website,
the search engine may not crawl the majority of your pages.

72

Kick the Orphans Out

You gotta be cruel to be kind (to your website). When requesting free or paid links from compatible web-sites, don't accept the lonely orphan link to your site. Instead, request links embedded within a family of rich text words related to the content on your landing page. Make sure the links are surrounded by rich content that works in concert with the optimization strategy of your landing page.

73

No Fishy Links

The words around a link phrase help the search engines resolve questions of ambiguity and equivocation. For example, in the sentence, "I'm a fish out of water here, but I'm learning how the place works," the isolated link phrase, "fish out of water," could refer to either a newcomer or a salmon. The other words in the sentence resolve the ambiguity and validate the meaning. When you're engineering link strategy, craft words around link phrases that support the SEO strategy of the landing pages.

74

Links: Think Inside the Box

Too many websites miss the opportunity to build link strategy within their sites that can support the optimization strategy of the landing page. Capitalize on this missed opportunity by making sure you have keyword-rich, contextual links to your internal pages. Contextual validation can start within your own website.

Beware of Tracker IDs

Sure, tracker identification on links helps you measure
conversion and sales, but the best links to your site are direct
links without any tracker ID in the URL. Why? Because the spider
bots quickly detect likely "profit measurement" from the link
and lessen the value in comparison with natural links—a major
disadvantage. In order to get something (more organic traffic
from the search engines), you may have to give something up
(accountability of your links).

Poison Kills

Improving your link popularity should have an impact on your
listing positions in the search engines, but make sure your
website is free of poison that can kill the boosting potential of
links. Common problems include unreadable menus, poor meta
strategy, broken links, temporary redirects, lack of site map,
poor navigation structure, and unfriendly session ID URL strings.
Tip your white hat too much, and it turns black.

Remove the guesswork of content marketing with A/B and Multivariate testing. Make your content and landing pages better—and then better than that.

Content Testing

Basic Landing Page Design Tips

Feature This.

We hate to be obvious, but you have to be obvious. When you design your landing page, be very obvious about your features. A reader shouldn't need a map and a flashlight to find what he or she is looking for. Use standard conventions as well, like bold, italics, highlights, hand-drawn annotations, iconic design, and more. You only have one chance to hook a passing reader, so say what you mean.

F-Bombs?

And now a few F-words. Research shows that web users tend to read through web pages in an F-shaped manner, so keep important images Flushed left. Put your most important information—your message, other copy, or hero-shot image— near the middle of the page (the lower prong of the F). If something is not important, move it to a sidebar or take it out. Always make Friends with your readers. One big way to be user-Friendly is to minimize the number of Fonts you use on a page. Poor type design is a visual turn-oFF. Cleaning up the type variations helps drive readers to the headlines and calls to action quickly. Try to stick with one Font, and don't bounce around between sans seriF and seriF Fonts.

Get the Picture

Not all pictures are worth a thousand words—some are worth
squat. The question is, how can your images best support
action on your website? Experiment with different images as
much as possible, tapping into seasonality, special occasions,
and other items that make your site feel in-tune and anything
but static. Custom images can outperform stock images, if
created in the right way. Stock images must often be used
and are a good way to test a layout before you create your
own custom images. Try using stock photography that is off
the beaten path, and manipulate the images you purchase
to make them stand out from the pack and fit the design of
the page. Images of groups tend to out-perform individual
shots, according to research, but experiments are the only way
to confirm whether an image will resonate with your target
market. When connected to your sales message, headlines,
and copy, abstract images can work as well, as long as they're
attention-grabbing. Try captions under images, zoom in and
zoom out features, call-outs, and text pointers in images. Also
experiment with attention-grabbing shapes like starbursts,
banners, and stamp effects.

Make it Look Easy

It pays to be a simpleton. If your landing page is text-intensive and MUST be text-intensive, then be sure to simplify your design. Use a one-column format and light colors (white works best) to raise readability. Also, break up large paragraphs in order to make the reader think that he or she's reading less than he or she is actually reading. If a paragraph or page looks too dense, readers will skip it, so make sure that all text is in small paragraphs (only about five lines) when you optimize landing pages.

Don't Send Them Away

It's tempting when optimizing landing pages to experiment with moving readers to off-page links with new tests related to the link phrase. Instead, use new browser windows for new pages or supplemental information or downloads. Define the purpose of the page and stick with it, using as few outbound links as possible. Better yet, avoid outbound links and pop-up pages altogether. Are we on the same page now?

The Top 300

We're not talking about Spartans. The internet is a very visual medium, so use that to your company's advantage. On your landing page, place your most important elements in the top 300 pixels of the page. Research proves that over half of site visitors do not scroll down. Remember that landing pages are not essays; they don't need any introductions. Get right to the point and put all of your most valuable information at the top of the page. Your sales will be tops.

Form Matters

Of course, it's all about the conversion—that's always what matters most. The more you can strip down your lead generation forms, the higher the conversion rate. It's really that simple. Make your site's forms easy to use. Making the input cursor automatically hop from box to box, allowing tabbing, or only using checkboxes are all excellent ideas for landing page optimization. Auto-filling form data set-up is an essential feature as well. Make sure to test your forms in different browsers. Talkin' 'bout lead generation.

Let the Customer Decide

Let's face it—everybody's a designer and copywriter. Everyone loves to form an opinion on which design or solution is better, but the key to landing page optimization is to put the customer in control. Your obligation is to not form an opinion and to test "just to see what will happen." That might mean radical price variations or stripping down the offer details. Test, then test again, then test some more.

Let Everybody Play

Landing page testing is exciting for companies, particularly with so much on the line. Circulate the choices among all employees of your company if you can and let them try to predict the winner. You'll probably be amazed at the lack of ability to predict successfully, but more importantly, you might just find "winners" in your office who can offer feedback and ideas in the future for testing.

Make It Snappy

On the web, it's lack of speed that kills. Visitors to your landing page can't wait to see it. If the page doesn't load quickly, they'll probably try a different site. In this era of high-speed internet, this isn't always a problem, but there are still millions of people using dial-up. For them, and in those instances when high-speed runs slowly, try for an eight-seconds-or-less loading time. Take out large, unnecessary graphics and optimize your landing pages so that the necessary images are of reduced file sizes.

Try Anything

Loosen up! Let yourself go! Wear your shoes on the wrong feet! Traditional landing page design usually offers navigation structure in the left column and support for the call to action in the right column. Try variations when you test. Move the navigation to the right column and add testimonials in the left column. As a second experiment, move the navigation to the bottom of the page, or delete it altogether. Experimentation is the key to layout—and success.

Outsmart the Competition

When looking for ways to improve the design of your professional landing pages, look at the competition. Carefully analyze their layout, flow, and conversion process, and if you find yourself getting confused or put off, make a note of why. Then, go back to your own site and compare designs. If you find the same problems, remove or revise them. It's a clever way to turn your competition against itself. (Just hope your competition isn't reading this.)

How Long Should You Test?

How long is too long? Why not find a quick winner and deploy that solution quickly across the board? Many reasons. Many variables can influence conversion rates, such as seasonality, time of day, economic situations, competitive positioning, source of traffic, and dozens of others. In addition, the volume of traffic on your site has a bearing on length of time to test. Here's our advice: use a statistical tool to crunch the data and offer the correct mathematical answer.

Your Customers Have the Answers

The customers who purchased from you or signed up with you are the best source for knowledge on how to motivate the sale. Too often, clients overlook this opportunity to ask them about their decision and the process. Take a look at Survey Monkey, an industry leader, for plug-and-play survey technology that will get you the answers you need to get under the skin of your target audience.

Avoid Shopping Cart Abandonment

Letting your customers know how long the checkout process is and exactly where they are in the process is paramount for success. One of our clients left out one of the progress indicators in the checkout process; in this case, it was a page for giving away free samples. By removing this step altogether, abandonment lowered and conversions improved. By adding the indicator on the step and placing it back into the cycle, abandonment lowered and conversions improved even more. Go figure.

Research of the retail environment, both online and offline, confirms that links back to product pages are important to a successful checkout gateway. Hitting the back button is viewed as risky by the consumer and fosters higher abandonment rates. Be sure that you have a thumbnail image of the product inside the basket and that it's linked back to the product page for further review.

Visitors may want to buy, but they don't want surprises. They do want answers to their questions along the way. The biggest question is: How much?

Showing inventory availability on the product page, rather than the shopping cart page, is also critical for reducing abandonment, and it also contributes to reputation management and word-of-mouth marketing. Both price and availability are part of the purchasing decision.

Include a prominent "Next Step" button or "Continue to Checkout" button on each checkout page. Also consider adding an "Estimated Delivery Date" and/or a "This product usually ships in X days" statement to help answer questions and eliminate anxiety.

If information is missing or filled out incorrectly, make it your fault during the checkout process bvy offering a meaningful error message that is visible and clear on the resolution.

Test offering contact information throughout the check-out process. By doing this, you'll let the customer know that you are a real company with a real phone number to contact for information. Use a different phone number to track these calls instead of the one on the main site that's used for tracking of behavior and test variations.

Improving Conversion Rates

92

Number, Please

Displaying a toll-free phone number on your site confirms that you're open for business. Try placing phone numbers in different positions throughout the site and varying the size of the phone numbers. Also experiment with the words around the phone number, which can make a big difference in how the target audience uses the number.

93

Live Help

Consider the amount of time you can support live help before you deploy the service. Also provide the service at the time of day that most conversions are made. If you have a 24-hour support plan, live help can greatly improve sales; however, success can be achieved without such service. Most importantly, test the technology yourself, ALL THE TIME from different browsers, IP addresses, and touch points. Live help that is not live can hurt your conversions greatly, so live it up!

Seals of Approval

BBBOnline certification seals, credit card logos, awards, media recommendations, Verisign and Hacker Safe logos, and other logo certifications are proven to improve conversion rates. Hacker Safe, for example, claims a 15%-plus average increase in orders. Experiment with the sizes and positions of the seals and put your own experiments to work measuring the improvement in conversion rates.

Survey Says...

Guessing intentions is difficult to do. Consider using survey technology to learn the intentions of your readers and visitors. We recommend asking just a few questions to learn intentions and better understand how to motivate the action. Questions to consider asking include: Were you satisfied with your visit? Did you find what you were looking for? Did you like the online experience? Knowledge from surveys can stop the guesswork and help streamline the sales process.

The Secret Formula

Here's a little secret for you to explore with testing: Lay out your above-the-fold section of a page with a simple formula: Relevant Image, Strong Headline, Concise Body Copy. Experiment with variations with multivariate testing techniques, but keep the formula the same for a series of experiments. You'll find that this basic formula in tandem with other techniques outperforms other variations for many good reasons. Why? Basic design fundamentals come into play. When looking at an image, readers make a decision to stay or go in milliseconds. If you're lucky, they'll read a headline in the following few seconds, again making decisions along the way. If you're very lucky, the reader will read the supportive copy, but this typically applies to a very small percentage of readers. Pages on the web need to be tested.

Use Your Headline

Headlines need to express the benefits to the customer while avoiding features of the product or service. They should also motivate in some way, offering results and improvement of some kind. Proof needs to be on the page, helping to make the offer more believable and trustworthy, and specific benefits need to be explored in a variety of ways with tests and experiments that help identify the best motivators. Explore headline formulas in magazines and on the web. There is a science to headlines that you need to learn to be successful online.

Testimonials

There's no question that testimonials can earn trust and improve conversion rates. Most clients neglect the opportunity to experiment with placing testimonials in different locations with various point sizes, weights, and even color in the text. Also, few clients take the time build a pool of testimonials that is large enough to put the full power of testimonials to work in matching the industry, voice, and style of the prospective client and existing customer. The perfect match will improve conversion almost every time. Develop a systematic way to collect testimonials, then make the most of them.

Make Them an Offer They Can't Refuse

You need to really think outside of the box with offer experiments. Clients are often reluctant to experiment radically, and as a result miss a huge opportunity to discover new revenue models and advance sales exponentially. Variations might include guarantees, free trials, bonus offers, payment terms, buy now pay later, automatic renewal, discount for cash up front, first one free, referral commission plan, limited supply, free shipping, free installation consulting, free customer service for 90 days, reverse time clocks for order deadlines, offer end dates and times, inventory limitations, lowest price matches, unconditional money back guarantees, warranty backers, volume discounts, free X with orders over Y, no-questions-asked return policy, and more. The key is to test as many offer experiments as possible in conjunction with different headlines, copy, and graphics on a page.

Testing Methods and Techniques

100

Make News

Getting your company in print and promoting the media source adds instant credibility to your company. Work creatively to get the word out—and the media coverage in—about your business. Craft press releases that offer the full story and make yourself available for comments on industry news. Open up this line of promotion with professional help from PR firms or tackle it on your own. Offer free trials of your product or service to the media with the hope of getting coverage in return.

101

Calls to Action

The all-important (and much-discussed) call to action needs experimentation more than anything on your website. You need to experiment with the words, the color and size of the type, and the graphics of the but- ton or icon used for action. In our opinion, you just can't test enough variations, even if you dedicate only 20% of your traffic to pure experimentation forever.

102

Coupon Codes

Be careful how you handle coupon codes on your website. Experiment with the offer to be sure that you are not decreasing conversion rates and adding confusion to the conversion funnel. Coupons should add to the experience, not create doubt for those who may not be shopping with a coupon and feel like they're leaving money on the table.

The Body Copy Debate

Content depth is required for conversion—it's that simple. Start by developing personas to learn who your customers really are and what they really want from you. This helps you persuade better. Often, each persona has different content needs. The process surrounding the sale also needs to come into play; it's a matter of a complex, five-step sales process vs. a one-step answer to the question. Speaking directly to customers will make them more willing to buy or take action. Also, lay out content so that it's skimmable and scannable by using bold type, italics, and highlights when appropriate. As for the length of copy? The debate continues, with testing variations being the only cure for the insanity. Test. Test. Test.

Multivariate Testing

Multivariate (or multivariable) testing allows you to test many experiments simultaneously within a single page and identify the impact of each individual change. Images, headlines and body copy are mixed, paired, and viewed in a variety of ways, with technology tracking the performance of each of the multitude of variations. With greater creative latitude, you can broaden the discovery process for finding the best path for conversions. It's a great way to dramatically and quickly improve performance on your website and in your email messages; however, the greater the number of variations, the more time required to get a statistically valid sample of visitors to achieve valid performance measurement.

A/B Split Testing

Simple, efficient, and fast, A/B testing allows you to compare a baseline control sample with a variety of single variable experiments to improve conversion rates. A classic direct mail tactic, this method of testing is easy to deploy and is a great starting point for testing copy, layouts, images, and colors. Experiments are typically distributed equally with the original control sample. Conversion results are measured and tracked for comparison and performance analysis. This method is different from multivariate testing, which applies statistical modeling for experimentation with multiple variables within the distribution.

Usability Tests

Web usability is an approach to make it easy for a reader to intuitively take action on a web page without ambiguity of consequence of action. Best practice usability methodologies maintain a straightforward and concise presentation of information, offering clear choices in an obvious way, with the most important information in the right place on a webpage or web application. Usability testing is part of A/B and multivariate testing methodology and is aimed toward narrowing down the most efficient placement of information to improve performance and conversions on a page. Eye tracking is used in usability testing, and KISS (keep it simple, stupid) principles are advocated by web usability experts.

Template Variation Tests

Experimenting with template layouts can increase conversion
significantly, especially if your existing template is noisy,
cluttered, and confusing. To test template changes on a
dynamic site while providing a consistent look to users
across many pages, the testing framework needs to simply
be involved in specifying a cookie that the website code
then uses to choose a template. Here's how it works using
Google's Website Optimizer:

- Customer enters site; Google testing framework
  sends test "content."

- This content is a <script> block that calls a
  JavaScript function that sets a cookie if it does
  not already have a value. If that function sees that
  the cookie is being set for the first time, it will
  also reload the page so that the server can get in
  on the action.

- On a request from the browser, the cookie should
  be tested for and the selection of the template
  should be changed accordingly. If the template is
  no longer valid (after the test cycle ends), then the
  default or current winner should be chosen.

- Even if that reader returns to the website, the
  cookies remember who they are and what
  template to display so that you can test and learn
  what works.

108

Eye Tracking

Identifying conversion-killing design and copy flaws is difficult to do. Sites may look great and perform poorly. We often discover that the problem is the grid system itself. Eye tracking and click tracking technology can help pinpoint the problems.

109

Click Mapping

Imagine a visual map that shows you exactly what readers view and click on your website before you even start the testing process. Before you try and modify the behavior, you really need to know what the behavior is so that you can work around the problems more easily. CrazyEgg is a service that allows you to supplement your analytics with cool visuals that help you take action more easily. ClickTale is another mouse-chasing platform that helps pinpoint behavior and improve usability on your site.

Landing Page Optimization Technology

SiteTuners.com has developed a proprietary technology dubbed TuningEngine. It is designed for very large tests (1,000,000+ variations) in high-traffic environments.

Formerly known as Offermatica, Omniture has a suite of services that includes testing technology. A pioneer in the multivariate testing space, the technology uses a modified version of the Teguchi method, which allows experiments with larger numbers of potential combinations to be run faster, since not all combinations have to be tested. They have a nice on-site visual interface that allows for marketers to create tests without any special configuration. Also, a nice profiling feature helps make it easy to get the right creative tests in front of the right target audience, at the right time.

Optimost's patent-pending technology is flexible and powerful enough to test any part of your website, including landing pages, web forms, dynamic product pages, and email campaigns. Segmentation criteria include, but are by no means restricted to, source of traffic, visitor demographics, cookie information, time/ season, behavior, and location.

Magnify360 is a web-based behavioral targeting platform. It builds and maintains comprehensive profiles of visitors based on 360+ dimensions, delivering the optimal landing page or website experience to every reader. The platform scores leads in actual dollar values, allowing you to calculate the true ROI of campaigns by day, week, or in total.

Website Optimizer, Google's multivariate and A/B testing tool, helps online marketers increase reader conversion rates and overall reader satisfaction by continually testing different combinations of site content (text and images). Website Optimizer is a free tool inside AdWords.

Content Distribution

Article Distribution

Article portals offer opportunities to get words out and links in. Guest posts are growing in popularity, creating a win-win opportunity for publishers and thought leaders to share information and advice. Beware of portals that have little or no editorial standards and exist primarily for link building strategy. If you do find e-zines with both quality content and authors, use traffic measurement as the guide for success, not page rank. Finding article distribution channels, portals and publishers is a manual process. But if you find the right partnership, you'll create an important distribution channel for content marketing success.

Annual Reports

Public AND private companies can both benefit from publishing annual reports. The allocation of resources and budget to share the past year's successes, milestones and accomplishments makes a powerful statement about your brand. After years of decline, look for digital and print annual reports to make a comeback. Explore this powerful storytelling channel to broaden your reach.

113

Awards

Winning awards in your industry for innovation, creativity, practices or growth is a great way to advance content marketing strategy. Find the awards in your industry and take the time to apply. Learn the details of what it takes to win, and reach out to the members, sponsors and judges as part of your strategy. Publishing the award banners and icons on your site and your content assets helps to earn trust and turns browsers into believers, and believers into buyers.

114

Guest Blog Posts

Guest blog posts are another important channel to help you establish your authority in the marketplace. It's a manual process to connect with publishers, nonprofits and information portals in your industry. For guest blogs, return on investment includes improved traffic, improved listing positions and even conversion enhancement if selected.

115

E-book Readers

Distributing content (like this book) to portable devices such as e-book readers is quickly growing in popularity. It's a great way to reach customers, readers and fans. Apple's iPad, Barnes & Noble's Nook, Amazon's Kindle, PocketBook and other e-readers are growing in popularity every day. And free tools like calibre offer open source e-book library management that helps convert e-books for use on portable devices.

Branded Content

Take a look at just about any print magazine these days, and you'll find a "Special Advertising Section" or "Promotion" section. These features typically offer informational articles and content provided or sponsored by companies that pay for the promotional service. Restrictions are often placed on the editorial quality of the content. But nowadays, with publishers scrambling for alternative revenue streams, many great opportunities exist for companies to reach new audiences with information that's indirectly related to their products and services.

Gamification

More than 70% of Forbes Global 2000 companies make use of game thinking and game mechanics in a non- game context to engage customers, solve problems and even attract new customers. Mobile applications are a big part of that surge in popularity, with applications that attract followers and fans in droves and lead to conversion and sales. Channels like Foursquare, iTunes, Facebook and Twitter make distribution fast and easy.

118

Mobile

Mobile marketing uses mobile devices, including cell phones and e-readers, as distribution platforms for any kind of promotion, including content marketing programs, information assets, games, advertising and more. Time- and location-sensitive information is particularly successful in this distribution platform, especially with personalized goods, services, offers and information generating value for all stakeholders. SMS messages are read on average within 4 minutes, making them highly convertible. Look for the IAB and MMA (Mobile Marketing Association) for guidelines and evangelization of this exciting platform.

119

Newsletters/RSS Feeds

Traditional print newsletters and leaflets may be a thing of the past. But email newsletters and RSS feeds continue to be the mainstream for many companies, schools, associations, clubs, churches, societies and any organization with subscribers, readers and fans. Don't miss this channel, especially if you have the resources to publish information that solves problems and entertains. Most content management systems and blogging platforms offer RSS feeds to opt-in subscribers and fans.

120

Magazines

The hype for custom publishing continues with companies that need to publish content on a regular basis. The Custom Content Council tracks developments in the field and confirms this distribution channel is growing in popularity. Magazines are a great distribution channel, especially if you have the resources and budget to create content that strengthens the relationship with subscribers, readers and customers.

121

Press Releases

Years ago, getting your story in front of the press and media was challenging. Hiring a PR company helped get your message on top of the stack. But all that changed with technology that helped get press releases out to thousands of media professionals. Optimizing press releases for SEO strategy is now common practice. New methods include embedded video, link building and social integration.

122

Podcasts

iTunes is one of the largest portals for podcast distribution, with hundreds of thousands of podcasts at listeners' fingertips. Podcasts are digital media consisting of episodic series of audio, radio, video, PDF or ePub files that are streamed or downloadable through web syndication.

Social Media (Not Blogs)

With readers orbiting at high speeds, distributing your content in the social sphere is essential. Twitter, Facebook and LinkedIn are core distribution channels for announcing the launch of new content assets and monitoring how they're received along the way. But that's just the beginning. Research which networks, portals and platforms are your customers', readers' and fans' favorite destinations.

Trade Shows (Virtual As Well)

Customers continue to gather at trade shows for that all-important face-to-face communication. Sure, people want to learn about new products and services. But they also want to find companies that solve problems and make work life smarter, better and faster. At your next trade show, focus on solutions to problems. And remember: Always present the information people want and need in a compelling way.

Content Performance

Performance Overview

Getting a firm grip on the impact of any content asset you publish is a must. Take the guesswork out of deter- mining content results by using the following ways to measure content performance.

Listing Positions

Given the speed with which consumers search for anything online these days and the handheld devices they use to do so, where your business appears on search engine lists, such as Google, Bing or Yahoo Search, is crucial. Original, compelling content drives listing position. Remember, if you're not listed on the first page of results, there's a dramatic drop-off of those willing to click to the second page and beyond.

Traffic

Just like a gas station on a busy highway, you need to know the path and measure the amount of traffic that's being driven to your business. By researching the search terms users employ to find you, future content can be created with the specific goal of increasing the traffic—number of viewers accessing your site—so that search engines deliver more.

Time on Site

Even though there are no clocks in a Las Vegas casino, don't think the house doesn't know how much time an average patron spends visiting his favorite game of chance. And in much the same manner, time on site is a measurement of the total time a visitor spends on your site. So when new content drives up the average time visitors are viewing your site, you can be confident you're on the right track to increasing business.

Repeat Visitation

It's predictable human nature that many visitors to your site will scan your content quickly at first before return ing a second or third time—and before taking some definitive action such as signing up, leaving a message or buying a product. Keeping track of the type of content that encourages repeat visitation, therefore, becomes a benchmark statistic when determining future content and planning specifically targeted business campaigns.

Clicks and Engagement

Until very recently, an online ad campaign's success was measured primarily by how many clicks—visitors manually clicking on the ad for more information—it generated. However, this statistic alone can be misleading. Engagement is the measurement of time users spend viewing, or being engaged by, a specific ad or piece of content. Nowadays, web savvy entrepreneurs know that the effectiveness of any digital asset isn't fully understood until both clicks and engagement results are considered. This is why creativity is still so important in building any brand's image, because it increases engagement. Otherwise simple large volume banners would be all you need to drive business. And seriously, when's the last time you clicked on one of those?

Downloads

We all like things for free, especially when they're chock-full of information about a topic, product or service that we want to know more about. This is why creating content in a downloadable format, such as an e-book, is a brilliant marketing move. By offering your customers, readers and visitors a way to find more about something they're already interested in, you can track the number of downloads, plus get more results and feedback from this engaged fan base.

Shares

People are talking all the time now via social networks like Facebook and Twitter, so why not make it quick and easy for them to talk about your business? The best way to do this is to add specific social media "Share" buttons obviously displayed on your site. Now you can sit back and see which pieces of content generate the most shares. Once you know what gets people talking, you can create future content that keeps the conversation going and growing.

User Acquisition Cost

Although at the height of the dot-com frenzy many businesses didn't look at the cost associated with generating new users, today's economically smart businesses need to carefully calculate the ROI associated with acquiring customers or users to their services and products. By adding up how much you're spending on research, content creation and marketing, and comparing it to how many new users you're acquiring and what their value is to your business, you'll be in a much better position to wisely plan future campaigns.

Page Views

Unlike merely measuring visitors to your site, page views
measure the overall number of pages on your site that are
clicked on. With this number in hand, you can compare
cumulative page views to your visitation numbers. And guess
what? If your page views remain higher than or increase
against your visitation totals, then you're creating content
that engages your readers—the all-important goal for brand
image and loyalty.

Conversion Rate

By employing tools like Google Analytics, you can track the
amount of visitors to your site who take a specific action like
making a purchase, joining a newsletter list or answering a
survey. In general, the percentage of viewers that takes an
action, or converts, is anywhere between 2 to 3 percent. So
any percentage higher than that is a good conversion rate,
and you know your content is having the right effect on your
target audience.

Customer Lifetime Value

The CLV, or customer lifetime value, is the estimated net profit a business can expect to make off an average customer, taking into account the predicted length of time that customer will remain in a business relationship with that company. In simple language, the longer a customer's lifetime is with a company, the more that company can afford to spend on advertising and special offers to retain that customer—hence why so many credit card companies throw out deals that seem to be too good to be true for the first year, or longer, that you use their services.

Content Marketing Tools

Social Tools

Search.Twitter.com

An easy-to-use search tool that allows you to find what people are tweeting about. Use this tool for competitive analysis, research or entertainment purposes.

IceRocket.com

Search in the Blog, Facebook and Twitter segments of IceRocket's search engine offerings. View top posts and searches or submit your own blog post into IceRocket's high-priority indexing queue.

TweetDeck.Twitter.com

A social media dashboard application that allows you to arrange your feeds into columns, filter and schedule your tweets to your specific audience, and manage your account and notifications with alerts.

Content Testing Tools

ConversionRuler

Measure the success and effectiveness of your online marketing with this monthly subscription service. With ConversionRuler, you can track your pay-per-click campaigns, banner advertising, and/or affiliate partner links. It also digs up the keywords people search when trying to reach your site.

VisualIQ

A cross-channel marketing attribution software that provides performance findings revealed from your marketing data. Specific features include the ability to discuss your needs with a VisualIQ consultant, sign up for an e-newsletter, or download an e-book.

Visual Website Optimizer

Increase your website sales and conversions with this optimization tool. Companies like Microsoft, Groupon and Mitsubishi use Visual Website Optimizer for A/B Testing, multivariate testing, behavioral targeting, heat- maps, usability testing and revenue tracking.

Mongoose Metrics

A phone call tracking and paid search phone optimization tool. This technology reveals the effectiveness of phone conversations with data from high volume enterprise call tracking to keyword level call tracking.

SEO Tools

Spyfu

Spy on your competitors' search marketing efforts with this tool. SpyFu allows you to see where they've shown up on Google, every keyword they've purchased on Adwords, every organic rank, and every ad variation in the last six years. Based on this data, you will receive recommendations to increase your website traffic and have the ability to track your keyword rankings.

Compete

Track and analyze your customers' online behavior with this tool. Through this digital marketing optimization tool, you can also learn what your competitors are doing by comparing conversion and bounce rates.

Quantcast

A tool that provides marketing measured data reports, including web traffic sources and frequency, website audiences and social demographics, as well as mobile web versus online visits.

SEOMajestic

A link intelligence database providing detailed information regarding your domain name, backlink history and link flow.

Raven Tools

Online marketers use this tool for building and assessing their marketing campaigns. This all-in-one software provides ways to manage and track SEO, PPC, social media and analytics effectively.

SEO Book

Work with and learn from SEO experts after signing up and joining this online tool. Membership includes hundreds of training modules and videos, a monthly SEO training newsletter, access to a community of SEO professionals and a communicative forum.

SEOToolSet

Enhance your SEO strategy and gain access to data reports with the available instruments and training programs offered by SEOToolSet SEO tools and methodology.

Link Vendor

Through this tool you can evaluate your SEO and social visibilities, analyze your site's effectiveness, manage your keyword positioning, assess your server and domain names, and utilize link tools.

Marketing Automation Tools

Act-On

"Marketing Automation for the Fortune 5,000,000." This sleek user interface offers tools for marketing automation, email marketing, lead management, landing pages, reporting and analytics, and social media.

Marketo

Used by small to medium-size businesses as well as global enterprises, Marketo assists in capturing and engaging leads through its software. Resources include e-books, cheat sheet guides, and success kits.

Eloqua

Power your revenue performance with this software, allowing you to provide a professional and personalized experience across channels, establish brand loyalty through social and online communication and relationships, and offer reliable customer service and support along the way.

Pardot

Using this tool, give your sales team the instruments they need to pinpoint the most effective leads and manage them; maintain a presence on social media with a steady publication of content; design and launch polished landing pages; create powerful email marketing; and know the true ROI of your marketing efforts.

Glossary

Abandonment

The number of people who begin an action on a website but fail to follow through with that action.

Above the Fold

Refers to the top portion of a webpage that is visible to the reader before he or she must scroll down.

Action

A specific action that a reader makes directly on a website. Examples include submitting an inquiry or purchasing a product.

Affiliate Marketing

A symbiotic online relationship between a company and a distributor. This usually involves an exchange of marketing products and services for a portion of sales or a fee.

Algorithm

A complex mathematical formula that uses weighted distribution to determine results. Many factors may be involved. Search engines, for example, include network theory, keyword density, linkbacks, global link popularity, longevity of the website, content changes, authorship status, and hundreds of other factors in the formula to determine results.

Below the Fold

The portion of a webpage that the reader must scroll down in order to see.

Call to Action

Copy that aims to elicit an action from the reader. Examples include "Find Out More," "Free Download," or "Test Drive Now."

Content

Anything included on a website that aims to attract and engage readers. Content refers to text, pictures, videos, sound, animation, etc.

Conversion

Causing readers to either buy or get closer to buying; turning a reader into a prospect or a prospect into a customer.

Corporate Blog

Blogging that allows a company to communicate its philosophy, personality, and goals to customers and prospective clients. Corporate blogging invites conversation between a company's employees, customers, and prospective clients.

Directory

A directory of websites that is constructed and maintained by human editors. Websites listed in directories are submitted by site owners and organized into categories. A directory usually only includes the higher- level pages of a domain.

Keyword Silo

The topic or theme for groups of keywords, utilized for purposes of the organization and development of your content strategy.

Landing Page

The page to which a reader is directed after clicking on an advertisement or link on a previous page. This is often the page by which conversion rates are measured.

Organic Listings

Free listings in the search engines that help readers find the right content for keyword phrases. Free listings also help websites drive traffic from the search engines for keyword phrases. Achieving top organic listings requires search engine optimization along with quality content.

Organic Market Share

This is focused on the amount of keyword phrases your business or organization is following or wants to rank for organically. Calculate the volume of searches for those phrases or terms, your ranking, and then operate a "potential" click-through metric to decide on the number of prospective visitors you would receive if you were ranking in the top three organic positions.

Persona

Types of people toward which advertisements, marketing campaigns, web pages, content assets, and more can be targeted; target audiences that share similar characteristics such as age, gender, income, etc.

Quality Link

A link that comes from a relevant source. Links are rated higher by search engines if the connections between them make sense rather than appearing forced or unrelated. Also, non-reciprocal links are considered of higher quality than reciprocal links.

RSS Feed

Short for "Rich Site Summary," RSS refers to a web feed that publishes regularly updated content such as a blog.

Social Bookmarking

Refers to websites that utilize reader response to highlight important content; often they provide buttons to make it easy for readers to bookmark the content on a social site (a personal blog or site).

Sponsored Listing

The title used to identify a listing as a paid listing or advertisement rather than an organic listing. Sponsored listings came as a result of a complaint that the lack of distinction between the two types of listings caused users to be confused and therefore qualified as advertising fraud.

Topic Map

Similar to a concept map, this tool organizes branches of knowledge into specific topics, giving structure to a project, like a blog.

Unique Visitor

An individual reader visiting a site, rather than a spider bot. Unique visitors are usually tracked by IP address and are counted based on the visit itself, rather than the number of links that they click within the site once they get there.

XML Feed

XML, which stands for Extensible Markup Language, is a scripting language used to transport data, rather than to display it (which is what HTML does). XML allows for the reader to define that data.

A site owner can submit an XML feed to search engines, which include the site in an XML-based search and assure regular crawling. The types of content covered by this method are expanding to video, audio, and graphics.

CPSIA information can be obtained at www.ICGtesting.com
Printed in the USA
BVOW06s2329110516

447619BV00004B/4/P

9 781602 750579